100
PRETENTIOUS
PROVERBS

First published 2002, reprinted in 2003 by
Prion Books Limited
an imprint of the Carlton Publishing Group
20 Mortimer Street
london W1T 3JW

ISBN 1-85375-486 2

Cover design by Grade Design

Printed and bound in Great Britain
by Bookmarque, Croyden, Surrey

100
PRETENTIOUS
PROVERBS

by Michael Powell

PRION

Pride comes before a fall.

A person experiencing a sudden drop from a relatively erect to a less erect position, should entertain the possibility that their inflated self-image is unendorsed by the general consensus.

A rolling stone
gathers no moss.

***

Never look a gift horse
in the mouth.

A hard non-metallic mineral rotating on its axis does not attract an accretion of cryptogamous vegetation.

***

Never perform an oscular examination on a gratuitous solid-hoofed plant-eating quadruped.

A stitch in time saves nine.

***

Many hands make
light work.

A sartorial procedure may be simplified by the timely and parsimonious application of a solitary suture.

***

Myriad manual appendages bring a salient levity to gainful employment.

A bird in the hand is worth two in the bush.

A feathered denizen of the sky, if manually restrained, could reasonably be exchanged for twain in the topiary.

People who live in glass houses shouldn't throw stones.

Inhabitants of vitreous structures of palpable fragility should refrain from lapidation.

All work and no play
makes Jack a dull boy.

If Jack is subjected to exclusively operose stimuli that preclude any recreational pursuits, he will exhibit oscitant behaviour.

Sticks and stones may break my bones but names will never hurt me.

Short lengths of wood and non-metallic mineral masses may inflict specific orthopaedic trauma but the use of onomastic syntax will never precipitate the onset of ontological distress.

Good things come to
those who wait.

Those who indulge in delayed gratification often accrue entities of a desirable nature.

Don't count your chickens
before they are hatched.

Aviculturalists should refrain from enumerating any gallinaceous livestock that still occupy their oval reproductive bodies.

Don't cry over spilled milk.

Forbear lachrymation with reference to lactose-rich beverages which have suddenly and involuntarily made contact with the ground.

A watched pot never boils.

Whether or not a heated liquid reaches its gaseous state is contingent upon the visible electromagnetic radiation from the cooking vessel reaching the retina of a sentient being.

More haste, less speed.

An increase in the precipitance of a given action results in an exponential reduction in performance (which often equates to the distance travelled divided by the time).

A man's home is his castle.

The physical structure within which all adult male humans are customarily domiciled can be said to resemble, in a metaphorical sense, a large ornate and fortified building such as Balmoral.

He who laughs last
laughs longest.

The individual who postpones risible behaviour until his contemporaries are expressing mirth by a series of spontaneous unarticulated sounds and corresponding facial movements, will blithely continue this restorative therapy for the greatest duration.

Look after the pennies
and the pounds will look
after themselves.

Parsimonious supervision of coins of small denomination will be rewarded with a sizeable quantity of the basic monetary unit of the United Kingdom (and Scotland before the Act of Union in 1707).

A nod is as good as a wink to a blind horse.

An affirmative lowering and raising of the head is equivalent to a deliberate closing and opening of the eyelid of one visual organ as regards a solid-hoofed, plant-eating equine quadruped, which, like Homer or, any of the various nocturnal flying mammals of the order Chiroptera, is destitute of the sense of seeing.

Never judge a book
by its cover.

You would be ill-advised to form an opinion or estimation of a set of written, printed, or blank pages, fastened along one side, based solely on your perception of its protective binding or enclosure.

Home is where the heart is.

A valued place offering security and happiness can be identified by locating the chambered muscular organ that maintains the flow of blood through a person's entire circulatory system.

Every cloud has a
silver lining.

The extremities of every visible body of very fine water droplets suspended in the atmosphere at high altitude consist of a lustrous white, ductile, malleable metallic element.

Charity begins at home.

Benevolence or generosity toward others, or toward humanity in general, originates in a dwelling place that affords comfortable and secure residence for an incumbent individual or social unit.

Make hay while
the sun shines.

Cut and dry grass or other plants, such as clover or alfalfa for fodder, whenever beams of light and other radiant energy emitted by the star around which the earth orbits is not obscured by visible bodies of very fine water droplets suspended in the atmosphere.

The grass is always greener on the other side.

Much slender-leaved herbage elicits in an observer the uneasy feeling that it possesses stronger characteristics of the verdant portion of the visible spectrum when it is situated on the less accessible of two or more contrasted areas.

You can't teach an old dog new tricks.

Reason recoils from any endeavour which seeks to add neoteric skills to the existing knowledge base of a septuagenarian Shitsu.

Man cannot live by bread alone.

A staple food made from flour mixed with other dry and liquid ingredients, usually combined with a leavening agent and kneaded, shaped into loaves and baked, when used as the sole source of nourishment for an adult male human, will sustain his life only for a relatively short period of time.

Do not throw pearls before swine.

Smooth, lustrous deposits of calcium carbonate, formed around specs of foreign matter in the shells of certain molluscs, should not be placed at the disposal of omnivorous, even-toed ungulates of the Suidae *family.*

Let sleeping dogs lie.

Resist the urge to interfere with canids luxuriating in the periodic state of rest indicative of their recumbent posture.

Beauty is only skin deep.

Even those blessed with pulchritude can be curtailed of their fair proportions by removing the surface of the membranous tissue which forms their external integument.

It never rains but it pours.

Water condensed from atmospheric vapour and falling in drops only ever flows torrentially.

Blood is thicker than water.

The fluid, consisting of plasma, blood cells and thrombocytes, that circulates through the vascular system of vertebrates – especially those connected by kinship – has a higher viscosity than a clear, colourless, odourless and tasteless liquid compound of oxygen and hydrogen.

Curiosity killed the cat.

Despite its apocryphal ability to cheat the machinations of the Grim Reaper, the life of many a small feline mammal has been tragically curtailed by its inquisitiveness and quest for knowledge.

There's no time
like the present.

The moment perceptible as intermediate between the past and the future appears to be the most favourable within the nonspatial continuum in which events occur in apparently irreversible succession.

One man's meat is another man's poison.

Fillet mignon belonging to an adult male human may produce disease conditions or tissue damage in a second adult male human with a non-identical physiology.

The pen is mightier
than the sword.

An instrument for writing or drawing with ink is more potent and efficacious than a long, straight or slightly curved, pointed blade set into a hilt (except in combat conditions).

You can't make a silk purse
out of a sow's ear.

A female hog's aural appendage should not be used as a cheap substitute for fine lustrous fibre produced by certain insect larvae, if one wishes to construct a Fendi bum bag.

Time heals all wounds.

The nonspatial continuum in which events occur in apparently irreversible succession from the past to the future will restore a person to physical and spiritual wholeness.

Beggars can't be choosers.

One who solicits the string with which a malignant destiny directs the actions of its puppets, forfeits all power of volition.

Silence is golden.

The absence of sound, or the condition or quality of being or keeping silent, is as gratifying as a soft, yellow, corrosion-resistant, malleable and ductile trivalent element.

Birds of a feather
flock together.

***

A leopard cannot
change its spots.

Warm-blooded, egg-laying vertebrates of similar plumage will live gregariously.

***

A large, ferocious cat, Panthera pardus, *wears nigrescent punctation it is powerless to transmute.*

If the cap fits, wear it.

If the head covering is congruent with the circumference of your skull, appropriate it for the protection and adornment that it provides.

There's no smoke
without fire.

There can be no vaporous system of small particles of carbonaceous matter in the air without a rapid, persistent chemical change that releases heat and light during the exothermic oxidation of a combustible substance.

The best things come
in small packages.

***

Walls have ears.

Those entities most positive or desirable in nature always occupy wrapped or boxed objects of below average size.

***

Upright structures of masonry, wood, plaster or other building material are equipped with (albeit invisible) organs capable of perceiving sound.

It is easier to forgive
than to forget.

Drawing a line is easier than drawing a blank, since excusing a fault or an offence, and renouncing any residual resentment which it may have engendered, can be accomplished with greater ease than banishing it from one's conscious thoughts.

Do not wash your dirty
linen in public.

When cleansing contaminated Calvin Kleins, avoid the laundrette and the consequent scrutiny of all the world and his canid.

Cold hands, warm heart.

Magnanimous individuals invariably betray the fact that the measure of the average kinetic energy of the particles in the chambered muscular organ which maintains the flow of blood through their circulatory system is somewhat higher than temperate, by not wearing gloves.

Do not kill the goose that
lays the golden eggs.

If you have in your possession a wild or domesticated water bird of the family Anatidae *which is capable of generating oval thin-shelled reproductive bodies of a soft, yellow, corrosion-resistant malleable and ductile trivalent element, under no circumstances should you cut it open.*

Better the devil you know.

***

Bad luck comes in threes.

A subordinate evil spirit with whom you are relatively well acquainted is preferable to one to whom you have not been formally introduced.

***

The relationship between individual chance occurrences of adverse events is always triadic (but not de facto one of mutual dependence).

A closed mouth
catches no flies.

***

May as well be hanged
for a sheep as a lamb.

Taciturnity inhibits the oral incursions of certain two-winged arthropods.

***

It behoofs a person to be executed by suspension on account of an ovine ruminant that has been weaned in preference to one that has not.

In the country of the blind,
the one-eyed man is king.

In a nation with exclusively sightless citizens, a male human need only possess a single fully functional organ of vision to attain pre-eminence.

Actions speak louder
than words.

Accomplishments can articulate with greater amplitude than sounds or combinations of sounds (or their representation in writing) that symbolise and communicate significance.

Don't put all your eggs
in one basket.

Forbear storing an entire collection of gallinaceous gametes within a single reticulate container.

Rome wasn't built in a day.

The design and construction of the buildings of the capital city of Italy was not accomplished within a single 24-hour period during which the earth completed one rotation on its axis.

Too many cooks
spoil the broth.

When a consommé is created by a surfeit of individuals specialising in food preparation, the result will be substandard and even unpalatable:
'cordon bleuargh'.

The early bird
catches the worm.

That shrewd, warm-blooded, egg-laying, feathered vertebrate which matutinally forsakes the pleasurable ease of its abode will ensnare a vermiculate creature.

Love is blind.

A deep, tender, ineffable feeling of solicitude toward a person or thing is incompatible with the possession of fully-functional organs of vision, and makes impossible anything other than the expedient idealisation of the percept.

While the cat's away the
mice will play.

The absence of a small carnivorous mammal, Felis catus, *will allow any of the numerous small rodents of the families* Muridae *and* Cricetidae *to occupy itself in amusement, sport or other recreational pursuits.*

No pain, no gain.

Nothing worthwhile is achievable without the release of peptide hormones and adrenalin into a person's brain, triggered by an unpleasant sensation occurring in varying degrees of severity as a consequence of injury, disease or emotional disorder.

Seize the day.

Take quick and forcible possession of the current 24-hour period during which the earth is completing one rotation on its axis.

If you can't stand the heat,
get out of the kitchen.

A person unskilled at thermoregulation, should seek employment outside the catering industry.

Money makes the
world go round.

That which Schopenhauer described as 'human happiness in the abstract' is responsible for the earth's vertiginous motion.

Mad dogs and Englishmen
go out in the midday sun.

Manic canids and male native inhabitants of England expose themselves mid-diurnally to pernicious solar radiation.

In for a penny,
in for a pound.

In for a coin used in the United Kingdom of Great Britain and Northern Ireland since 1971, worth one hundredth of a pound, (or a discontinued coin formerly worth one twelfth of a shilling or one two hundred and fortieth of a pound), in for the basic monetary unit worth one hundred new pennies (or 20 shillings or 240 old pence pre-decimalization).

Do not bite the hand
that feeds you.

Refrain from inflicting mordant discomfort upon a manual appendage which displays nourishing beneficence.

A heavy purse
makes a light heart.

When your Dolce & Gabbana porte-monnaie is pregnant with 'coined liberty' (to quote Dostoevsky), your chambered muscular organ will maintain the flow of blood through your circulatory system with palpable levity.

As you make your bed,
so you must lie in it.

The arrangement of rectangular items of insulation on a piece of furniture designated for sleeping will determine one's degree of comfort when palely loitering.

Cross the stream
where it is shallowest.

Do not essay the briny swell of the Hellespont but seek instead safe passage where the water trickles like Niobe's tears.

Every man is his
own worst enemy.

Every adult male human feels hatred toward and intends injury to, or opposes the interests of, himself.

Give a thief enough rope
and he'll hang himself.

Offer a kleptomaniac a sufficient quantity of flexible heavy cord, and you furnish him with a snuffer to quench the earthly lantern in his troubled soul.

It is too late to lock the
stable door when the
horse has bolted.

It is ineffectual and obtuse to make secure the movable structure used to close off the entrance to a building for the shelter and feeding of a solid-hoofed, plant-eating equine quadruped, subsequent to that animal's abscondment.

The last straw breaks
the camel's back.

When a humped, long-necked ruminant mammal of the genus Camelus *has suffered a severe dorsal injury, the cause can invariably be identified as the single stalk of threshed grain that was most recently added to a large accumulation.*

Marriages are
made in heaven.

The legal union of a man and woman as husband and wife is manufactured in the sky or universe as seen from the earth, which some believe is the abode of God, the angels, and the souls of those who have attained salvation.

One man sows
and another reaps.

One adult male human scatters seed over an area of land designated for arable agriculture, and a second adult male human distinctly different from the first will cut the grain or pulse at the appropriate harvest time.

Rats desert a sinking ship.

Those fickle and expedient rodents of the genus **Rattus,** *have a tendency to disembark from any sailing vessel of considerable size that is in the process of descending to the bottom of a given body of water.*

Spare the rod and
spoil the child.

The oversolicitude displayed by the decommissioning of the birch arms a person 'twixt birth and puberty against the vicissitudes of life with nothing more than an ungenerous nature and a misbegotten sense of morality.

There's many a slip
betwixt cup and lip.

A considerable number of accidents occur when a small open container used for drinking is in the process of being manually manoeuvred towards either of two fleshy folds that surround the opening of the mouth.

Tomorrow never comes.

The 24-hour period during which the earth will complete one rotation on its axis, which follows the present 24-hour period during which the earth completes one rotation on its axis, never occurs in the non-spatial continuum in which events take place in apparently irreversible succession.

Two's company,
three's a crowd.

Intimacy may be missed when a tryst becomes triadic.

You cannot put an old head
on young shoulders.

It is unwise to transplant the uppermost or forwardmost part of a body exhibiting the wisdom and maturity of age between the neck and upper arm of a person in an early period of development.

You can lead a horse to
water but you can't
make it drink.

A solid-hoofed, plant-eating equine quadruped can be successfully accompanied to a given quantity of a colourless transparent liquid compound of oxygen and hydrogen, but may nevertheless exhibit acute hydrophobic pathology.

You must lose a fly
to catch a trout.

It is necessary to forgo the companionship of a two-winged insect to capture freshwater or anadromous fish of the family Salmonidae.

Don't cut off your nose
to spite your face.

Refrain from amputating the part of your anatomy that contains the nostrils and organs of smell if your sole motive is to inflict malicious humiliation upon the front of your head.

Don't teach your
grandmother to suck eggs.

Do not patronise the female progenitor of either of your parents by offering tutelage with respect to drawing oval thin-shelled reproductive bodies into the mouth by means of intermittent movements of the tongue and lips.

Fools rush in where
angels fear to tread.

Those deficient in judgement hasten negligently in circumstances where, by contrast, benevolent celestial beings are indisposed to any pedal movement.

All that glisters is not gold.

Everything that scintillates with effulgence is not ipso facto *a soft, yellow, corrosion-resistant, malleable and ductile trivalent element.*

Many a true word
is spoken in jest.

A large though indefinite number of morphemes or combination of morphemes that symbolise and communicate meaning with unimpeachable veracity are articulated with the primary motive of eliciting a humorous response.

What the eye doesn't see,
the heart doesn't
grieve over.

The chambered muscular organ that maintains the flow of blood through the entire circulatory system can only be placed in a state of sorrowful distress if the electromagnetic radiation from a given object reaches the internal photosensitive retina of either of a pair of hollow structures located in bony sockets of the skull.

He that would have eggs
must endure the cackling
of hens.

Anyone wishing to accumulate oval thin-shelled reproductive bodies must be prepared to suffer patiently the shrill vociferation of gallinaceous livestock.

Life is not all beer and skittles.

The property or quality that distinguishes living organisms from dead organisms and inanimate matter, manifested in functions such as metabolism, growth, reproduction, and response to stimuli, does not solely consist of a fermented alcoholic beverage brewed from malt and flavoured with hops and a game played with nine wooden pins and a ball.

The road to hell is paved
with good intentions.

The general public way to the abode of condemned souls and devils and place of eternal punishment was constructed using a material of morally excellent objectives.

Little strokes fell great oaks.

Small indentations cause monoecious deciduous or evergreen trees of the genus Quercus *to undergo a sudden change in their spatial relationship with the ground, viz., from perpendicular to horizontal.*

Barking dogs seldom bite.

Domesticated canids which habitually utter a harsh sustained vociferation only infrequently inflict mordant damage.

Necessity is the
mother of invention.

The force exerted by circumstance is the female progenitor of mental fabrication.

A miss is as good as a mile.

Failure to accomplish or attain a goal is equivalent to 5,280 feet or 1,760 yards (1,609 metres).

None but the wearer knows
where the shoe pinches.

Only the individual who utilises a durable covering for the lower extremity of the leg can ascertain the narrowly particularised and localised position where the internal surface of that footwear presses painfully against the surface of his or her membranous tissue.

Lightning never strikes
twice in the same place.

An abrupt atmospheric discharge of sub-atomic particles never occurs in twofold quantity in a given locale.

Humorous quotation books by Prion:

Des MacHale
Wit
Wit Hits The Spot
Wit On Target
Wit – The Last Laugh
Wit Rides Again

Aubrey Malone
The Cynic's Dictionary

Michelle Lovric
Women's Wicked Wit

Rosemarie Jarski
Hollywood Wit

Look out for:

Michael Powell
High Society
Funny Money